KISS MY EARTH

First published in 2025 by Blue Diode Press
30 Lochend Road
Leith
Edinburgh EH6 8BS
www.bluediode.co.uk

All rights reserved. No part of this book may be reproduced, stored in a retrieval system, or transmitted in any form, or by any means, electronic, mechanical, photocopying, recording or otherwise, without prior written permission from Blue Diode Press.

© Alice Willitts

The right of Alice Willitts to be identified as author of this work has been asserted in accordance with Section 77 of the Copyright, Designs and Patents Act 1988.

ISBN: 978-1-915108-29-6

Typesetting: Rob A. Mackenzie
text in Minion Pro

Cover art: Alice Willitts
Cover design and typography: Theo Willitts

Diode logo design: Sam and Ian Alexander.

Printed and bound by Imprint Digital, Exeter, UK.
https://digital.imprint.co.uk

KISS MY EARTH

Alice Willitts

BLUE DIODE PRESS
EDINBURGH

to the restless, with love

Contents

9	She Finds It Difficult To Pray
13	April is High Summer in 2057
19	Her Strong Tongue
23	Still Moving
39	Robed
41	Womb Proverbs

> If there are always two ways
> to exist in time, as I've seen, one is denser, the other's told
> … I begin creation, but I'm not a god.

Alice Notley

> there is no angel to
> wrestle, there is no inter-
> mediary, there is something I must tell you

Jorie Graham

> For we are on the verge of losing this most precious and beautiful of worlds, a miracle in all the universe, a home for the evolution of souls, a little paradise here in the richness of space, where we are meant to live and grow and be happy, but which we are day by day turning into a barren stone in space… We can only make a future from the depth of the truth we face now.

Ben Okri

She Finds It Difficult To Pray

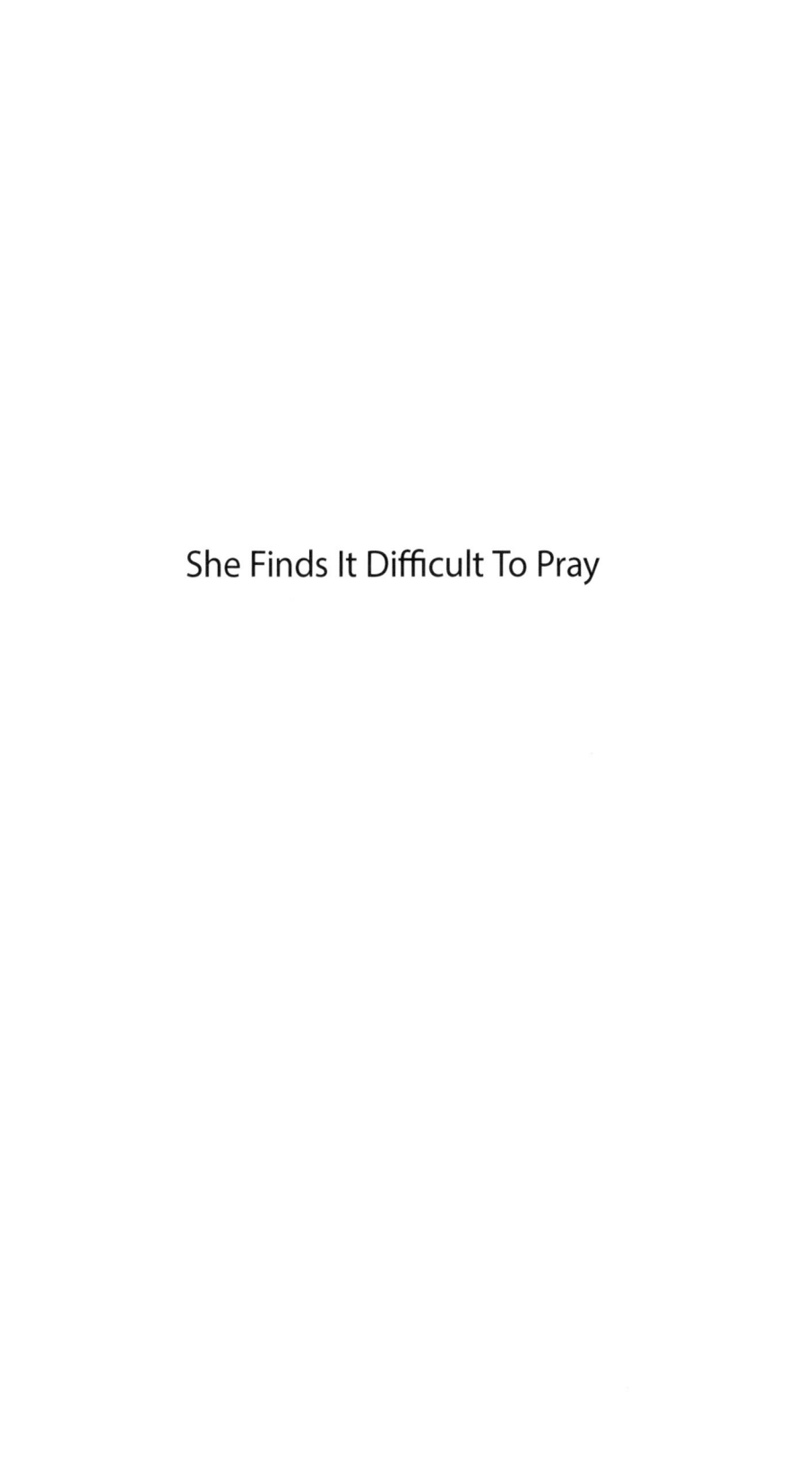

for Etheldreda, Queen of Northumberland and Abbess of Ely

wordsmith from drystones
        do you miss the fulmar shriek
hail-ice
at sea
        the limpet stack?

        you're on the fen now

call out loud   call full-throated
        we need a miracle
        we need to heal
our planet would a-wounding-go
the people are a-weeping

& the flood is coming
        women are closing up like bivalves
        women are clustering their babies

how did *you* pray up the storm?
        horses & armour chasing you down estuary
        foam & force & wicked fear

you prayed in a cave
        more a lowly scrape in the dunes
            cut off on the spit
        how did you pray up that storm?

if wanting is enough
make me the wilked wave & bruise the sky as I toss up
the enclosures
        of the sisters of the wives of the mothers
                of the muses of whatever they're calling us

I want to be a wilked wave
        wash away every address in a skeet sea
      reeve the land   until Ely floats
                              again &

Cambridge rowers will scull dons to a new shore
                        far above the bridge of sighs &
      I will swim down
      into the Library of Climatology
where octopus computers are tethered
flickering
      their one bewildered eye
after all, they knew—

water is the story

no matter the Mars men
let them rocket & waste up the speckled sky

wordsmith
        flanked by the bright shells of astronauts
tell me
if we could humble ourselves

flatten our bodies out   on the fen
                          like water does

what prayer is there now
that could lift up the ground on one side & pool us
                                & quickly

April is High Summer in 2057

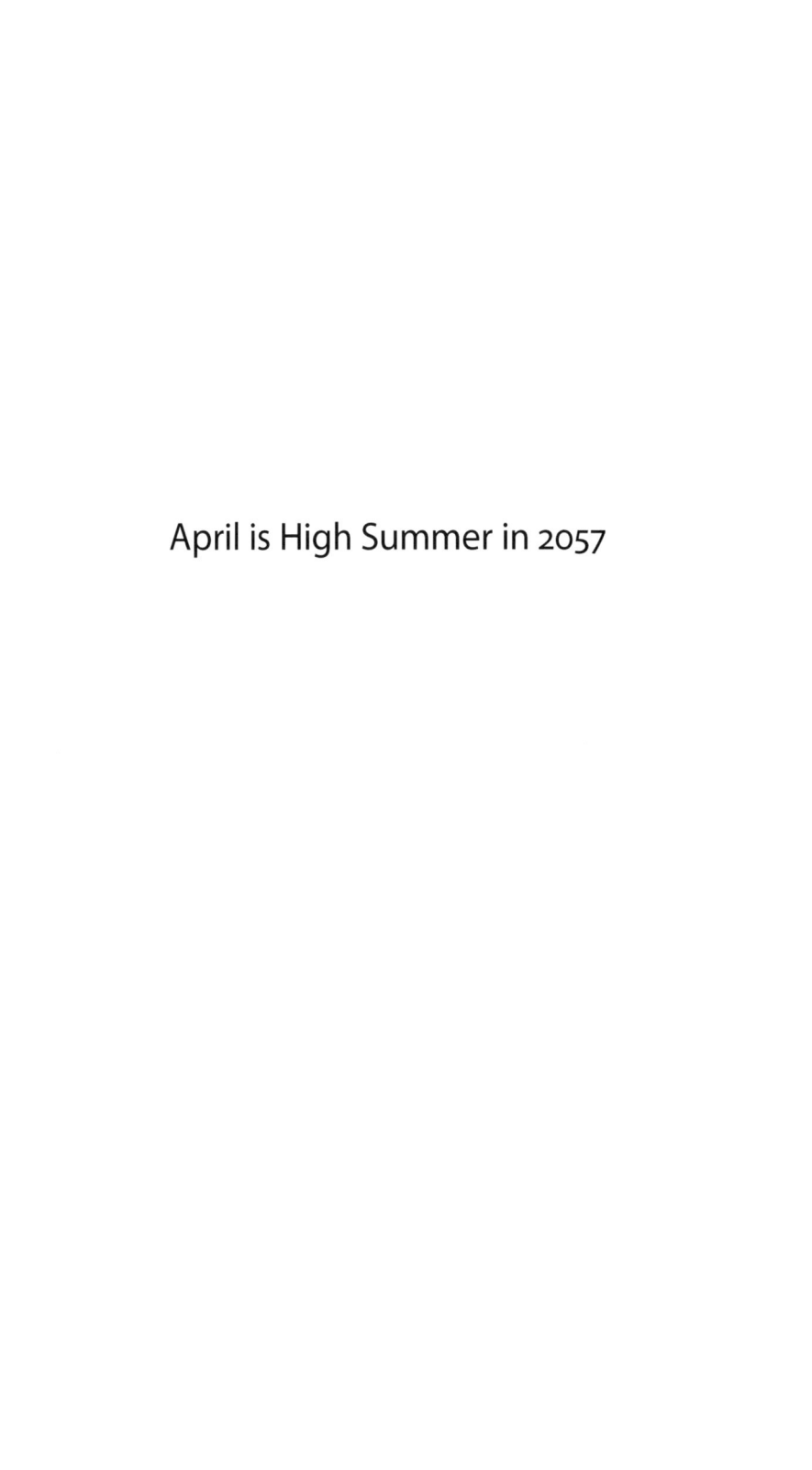

i. there is a new seashore in Cambridge; a closed door

lost children. hooded eyes a dust
kicking geography in circles
beating my womb so rounded
on a generation. i lean on seasoned
woodgrain. ash maybe. i count our
migrating footfalls in a kind of patience
travel on the smell. a salty flood
seeping back into my old garden. i miss
the simple hyacinth
pungent hippopotamus of flowers
friend a voice says *very little*
that is real just vanishes when it dies
no Alice you're wrong
remember how heaviness could
be dug from mud at Barrington
held in museums or hands.
the riven sea will be a scouring now
bones are selfless in two ways.
they're drowned again. there's a song
i know about love. its house is plain.
the ground is steady. the door open
but from the window the Cam laps up
new waves. dragging the poplars
still hustling a convincing river-
tongue along the bank we stood on.
swam off – before – we drifted in a clear
past charmed by our murmuring
soil – heart i said rock belly
head you said leaf hand cloud –
fleshed words quarrelling on & on

ii. there is the territorial blackbird; heat leaving the day; Jorie Graham, Alice Notley & Alice Willitts sit round the kitchen table in Hertford Street

we are stitching light to the wall. marking the year's days
    by their heat. a pattern of place
the plaster holds in seams and is creasing behind our needles
    like seersucker.

we stitch. regular work. in. out. dashes accumulate.
    murmuring stitches. slant
to where we were born. our landscapes or were they
    cities? winter. a small room. essential heat.
has fire ever not sung? our songs carry the sacred
    even though we are not all believers.
we task ourselves to carry belief home
    like birds sing themselves out & back daily.

when women were birds. sometime ago now. cracking
    ice-time & freeing squawks. our vowels
birthed on hilltop places. our wings taking moonlight
    smoothing vanes into blood in return for arms.
& isn't the feminine all arms anyway? how many times
    do we want to fly away?
lifting our arms. we hold winds. by binding
    women's arms we starve

chain link and running. we sew and stitch. regular work. say
    we kill their children. yes. with each baby we kill another.
isn't aggression towards ourselves the first war? say
    we are not killers. oh but we are. not en masse. but so regular
we carry the baby. we feed the baby. we hold the baby. we grow
    the baby to kill another baby. we are
responsible. we who are stitching our running voices
        stitching cloths for blood. monthly. asking

before man. how was the heavy flight of the bee
    timed. or the fern fronds. uncurling dew in their hundreds.
when we gaze across unfurling green we can be so fluid.
    moving without moving. transported. we say time is flying
where did the time go? like when a missile ticktocks borders
       we only name the impact. time has flown. our grasp of time
too human. the tracer glow of *storm shadow*
    another strike on our home. night closes on our voices

tomorrow we three. at my kitchen table on Hertford Street
    hunting for stories in seams. faces
can cry with other faces. we can. & do not
    mistake us for sentimental.
the blackbird knows its astonishing
    awl of sound. fears have taken nest in my mind.
& in my body. the baby stretches. plants a foot
on my rib. forward rolls. onto my cervix.

while in the mind a clock goes ahead
    still. we are all patterns. with other patterns.
a singular material woven from the finest loops of time
we stitch. to see ourselves made.
now i make tea & baby settles as i move around. breathe.
    rinse the pot. i want to tell you how *i think like tea sometimes
floating*. the baby as me. breathe. in rhyming ions.
    breathe. we wait. we sew. tea cools. breathe.

iii. here are raw materials

              your tiny arms fly outwards   surprised
by the vastness of your reach   they tremble   we all travel out
where we came in   at least once   to make that turning
& taste the first fungal mouth in a rush of fluid

slowed mucosal priming   ears rinsed of the heartbeat   fingers
in the touch of the other   a nose for air & a milk
mouth   skin to skin in your metallic scent   sweet

i am glued to this first marvel   like a drop of time
is hurtling from me to all the furthest places
right up close
        life's weave loops us   the pattern-making
animal   did image & sound start together
with the first cry? the first face?   us   cut

you & i were one fabric
& now? a seam feeds you
and i'm already sewing you   into place
even as the ruin of placenta follows you out of me

the space of my arms
              filled with your beauty is scarce
& you looking back at me   terrifies
such that carrying you

i am naked
        the sea has come to our door   naming us
    child & mother
such familiar sounds but lapping on soil
too soon for sand

though if i tell you these things
                it is to sew them into new cloth
chain & running   my feet nudge
the waves of the muddy shore   i'm looking out
at the alders & willows
i thought you would climb too
submerged
        their bare crowns
make me peculiar company

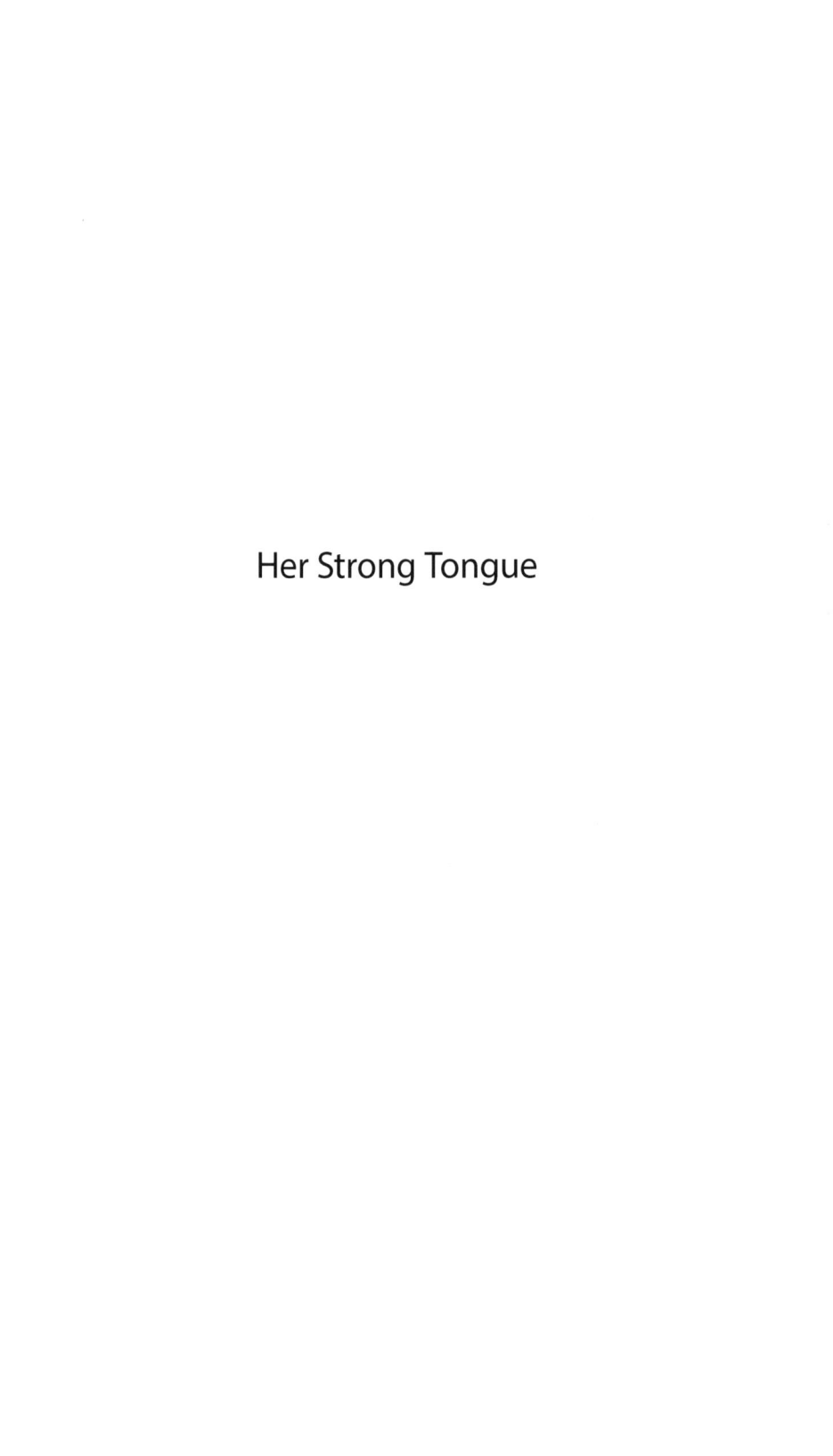

Her Strong Tongue

face down on black
damp Fen on my cheeks
on my chest my eyelids

on the soil. to roll in like a
pig with my orange bristles
rising on the cobbles of my

jerky neck. to snout the magnetic
mould of it bite in lick in till
I'm grit with it suck at the

gaps. where breath thrills
tongues of dirt
a commerce opens

>   between shame
>   and songs the faithful
>   kinfolk left, shifting longing
>
>   because what we cover
>   we consign to silence

wanting to forget an artist has
a body because my voice has
a fragile physique that sometimes

means motherly or can stutter,
not knowing how to hold
her strong tongue, still

tides in the solid
earth as in the oceans
detail the revolution

        but from far enough out
        everything appears
        still all the time

and me born in a city
that nibbles at baby lungs

cockchafer city nipping
roots of occupation
that were not mine, to live

on that balcony, a narrow curfew
which is small space
hanging off the edge of safety or

which I could feel again.
translate what whines
and hisses in my ears

or listen in at the mouths
or place my head oh gently!
on the belly of my sleeping boy,

        why ask for a chant
        while sirens
        are how we speak

a safety of quiet is no hurrying
only insect sounds and more than buzzing
there are two bees fighting

never heard that before
and red ant drags dead beetle
scraping its hard shell

over concrete,
muscular ant effort
a faint vibration at best…

all things must fall in elegant arcs.
think of it this way
there is no mistake

>	artists ask all the blushed
>	minerals for answers

>	thank the hands
>	that have forgotten
>	how to refuse

sleep is worth recalling
because there was a time
when we knew it

and now with paper maps
people are walking
backwards

Still Moving

so this is   it
               to lose language
in order to leave you

to stop talking
        cleanly
or neatly
but you don't anymore

say something back you say but there is
no back   there is
no say   you don't say
and I can't
say
something   the language has to fail us
torrents of failure
whole sodden libraries of it

        your pocket holds
all the damp tattered pieces
of my first sounds
in place

since   no   more
sense-making   the space
is taken

and plants' flexible stems won't write
time
we read their bending   as wind

my garden was not a garden
five hundred million years ago
it grew a third of the way down
from the equator towards
the south pole

up the way, at Barrington, fossil bones quarry
hippopotamus who wade the chalk-flat Cam
        as giraffe reach over
my children's climbing frame to the new
buds on the apple tree   lions hunting wildebeest
trample through my squash and cabbages

I'm not making it up

the radical geographer in the explaining part
of me
         steps up
she says, yes, of course
the solid soil of your garden moves
up and down like waves
         and I believe her

there is no stable part   look again
she says

and I do

my baby's eyes drift   milk-drowsy
lolling
back on herself   pulled under by what
waits inside
turning over in the stories as if we are all
living
at any one time

as if I could remake the world

I watch the soil rising___falling
like breathing
in the plants
in the very paths of the garden

I can breathe in soil   through the soles of
my feet
into my red spleen   up the heavy tackle
between my shoulder blades
and feel the ground   heave

there are voices in the soil
that I have sifted by hand
rolled in my fingertips
among the plants

voices who dry like lacy gloves in my creases

> I might know them
> *how do you do?*
> burrowed loam
> holding together
> the many volatile
> particulate traces
> of the dead
> chthonic wood-was
> echoes of another
> place a voice
> once twice released

        as if I can hear them
        troubling what exists
        in whispers not shouts
        sibilances of maybe
        my many-thousand-year-
        old-neighbour-selves
        their brief thoughts
        a clastic percolate
        to be turned out as a
        catastrophe of sound
        blushing in the deceptive
        hush of this suburban garden
        where they become   a din

        as if no trace of sulphur
o bright laburnum element!
        or trace magnesium
o kingfisher of metals!
        could illuminate the theory of place in this
        discrete handful of soil

I read the world   snipe-eyed

        dream earth   unstable
                       gasping under the
blanket
      of green stories

I am a moist absence
      suspended like fog

I look at   and past   not through the
world
as it reveals the thick bones
of itself   and in that most mort
                     silence
                     is the hot tunnel before
fainting

a seasick awareness

I am the word   in

pulling me   in
the soil curving away
picking me up
                         and I feel
frightened   new as the shock
of being carried on a riptide

I try tripping the word
as if it were more
solid in soil

      even the poetic garden blackbird
          chalking in the dawn cannot
not really

only later   I remember the advice is to float

our first elements
                are damp
babyish
birthed things
moisture first
breast first
our tiny fist
                soft
on the land

I emerged from an extremely hot and dense
small cluster
as a seed in mid-flight
          waving to mathematicians
          noting the point of me

during the whole arc
after I left home
I hadn't told the soil I was coming

no seed lets
the soil know
where it will land

childhood told me I stand in
told me that I am
in the garden
in love
in space

they said up   so I looked up
they said down   so I looked down
but was always a curve
falling in

you must know
when you look up
at the moon
you could be looking
down

yes, sky___space___universe is all over us
yes, even under your foot on the ground

what is it you think you're standing on?

wherever you stand
you are in
the falling

        we can't see the sound of voices
o joy of writing!
        we can't see the heat of bodies
o joy of touching!
        we can't see love
        so we give our little kisses

poor mute plants, why didn't I read them?
all that time   to exist   only as the old
men had told me

how unknowable they feel

these voices of the ground
answering an undulating naturalness
that is both
apparent and obvious

>   but how do I know it?
>   love is such a heavy
>   force   spinning
>   from normalcy all
>   folded in microbial
>   energy loosely
>   shaven clawing for
>   a foothold on scree
>   slipping and there is
>   no place to fault
>   the light consumed
>   by leaves   as if
>   the sky wasn't always
>   losing it

I cradle her tiny sleeping body

a chilling spot at the root of my skull
                           rolls with moon-gravity
night cannot snatch
the path
without your wilful blindness I tell myself

whisper it to me
night cannot snatch the path

I don't believe
my twenty-first century eyes   when they
show me
stillness___stability___solid___surfaces
because certainty
   is lawless now

but I
am still interested in
viability

a sharp flock of blue-tits
breaks the sick tilting

gratefully, gratefully

I simply see them
as I always have
        swift flurries of blue-yellow

        see? how they dip through all the
moving
        and make it look   still

Robed

If you wash your hands in the beak-sip of goldfinches,
in the slow-lap of bear, you wash dishes
in the call of red kites emerging from cloud,
and shower your body
in the flick of fish scale and pike tooth,
if you bathe your body in raindrops that fell once in China
on the head of six year girl on her way to school
if you rinse clothes in the dirt-splash of puddle water
thrown over a pavement and onto my legs in Tower Hamlets
I can conjure for you the cold shock,
the trickling down
inside shoes, the squelch between toes.

I wash myself daily in the water that your nanny
and her nanny drank and the rain
that pelts my mind today is all the fen's blackest crows settling
on my roof, cawing out chaos in the singular voice of water—
for I like to know who's speaking—
when I was sent away from my family
no one spoke my language. Fitting in is
like a dress, you put it on and try
copying their floating movements.
Belonging is a robe. When you step in
the robe is waiting to carry your body home.

Robed is crows making dust angels for each other,
taking tumbles in the dust, crying air for you;
Robed is attending fully to the business of
being; is this last labour, in this birth of yourself,
born into the beauty of elder flowering
and throwing off frills; we are not invisible
women are where we grow;
Robed is medium to fat and closed on Sundays to non-believers;
Robed is we're all soil worship now
but you cannot hear plants preach
if you believe they do not speak.

Womb Proverbs

my soft tongue breaks

In the electrified feathers of creation.
Soil's placenta receives and receives us. Air's
amniotic sac cushions us. And cushions us;

We can suck and swallow, frown and
stretch – yawn even, we are so blessed:

A low-down rolling sensation is
making some of us sit down sharply.

The people not to trust are five-faced.
With an expression of looking all ways at
once. East, South, West, North and Satellite:

And they think with their faces. Five-
faced-babies. Growing directly out of tech.
Their mantra. Never look down!

Precious. Fusty. Life. The humid
brown soil. Is deeply played. The rumble of
an organ base. Blowing air in the pipes of the
ground. Bellowing at the five-faced to stop!

Other voices vibrant with static.
Multiply like old man's beard. Become a
swamping lanugo on the bodies where
silence used to thrive;

Think of the five-faced like this. Their muck is pungent because they are host to a rare smut. A kind of incensed fungus. (And with no studies funded). We do not know. Where it will put down its tumorous musk foot. Where next.

how do we make sense of the losses? plants announcing themselves present only after they've left the building

Out in the garden. A scent of tar knocks over all the yellow. Right at my feet:

What can my eyelids do but play. At closing. As if. To not see. With all the seeing in me. Such a yellow want.

Go away five-face. With face on face on face on face on face I see you. Parting daisies with your claws. Your sterile satellite face. Has never looked so serene. Your suckle greedy. How you guzzle us.

Don't worry. The five-face say. In the end nature finds a way to let us know;

Quite by coincidence though the connection has come loose.

In my heavy womb. Clematis and feathers are so candid in their gestures to the wild. They are ungovernable embers. Starting something wherever and whenever they please.

I name myself an act of care. Holding our women's hearts up to a healing sunshine;

Let us come by again the morning after the burning. Nodding our dusty heads. As if somewhere in our cellscape. Might be how to rebuild without building. How to re-wild without any thing. Wild. Left in us;

So tame we kiss the wall. Bow our eyes to the satellite net. That never sets. Like heaven.

*I can be brain-heavy
as in too many synapses flickering gold in the
brown deep day*

I am a mother. Bent. Hunting the dykes
for a sweet medicine. A ripe salep from
tubers. Rooted out from that part you call
noise.

I am the part that sounds not unlike
the shriek of a nesting bird in the sightline of
a cat.

The five-faced only sing in tune
when Bitcoin is listening.

The People cheer for their
Soil-Free Field. Progress. Creepy sterile
rooms. Towers of tomatoes. LED lights.
Glowing lavender ambience. I fear the
banishment of bacteria. Like an evaporating
cloud. Blowing out of the blue sky of our
lives. Forever;

Then I hear the automatic timers
whispering.

The horror of The Indoor Field
scratches at my retina. I'm an old
etching plate.

I'm sorry___I'm sorry I say to the plants.
I'm sorry. For the plants;

    Plants who love the wind. Who love the gripping feet of insects. Love their mouthparts and rubbing thighs. Live for the low throbbing of a bee. Plants who long for the bodies of raindrops. A touch of dew to cool their racing pulse.

    Momentarily. A hard accuracy of guilt will peel out after the last tractor's silence. What was supposed to keep us alive.

    Mothers. High pitched and frantic is what I'm listening for. My sonic-aid. On the heartbeats. Fading. In the placenta of the soil.

extinction turns out to be the footsteps of children behind distracted adults

Morning of stars in lantern green. I lay
out my arm on the chest of the soil the way
ripe grass falls from the scythe. As in no skin
knows mine the way hay loves the soil it lays
on.

An ancient ridge in me is aglow. Out
by the blue shade. Out by too bright a start
for my bairn's tooth.

My fingers close on one patch of hairy
stem. And bend the hairs. And bend inwards
till they touch___release___I have, I have done
harm.

My dear body knows creation. My
body carries death. My body carries life.
Inside my own bloody womb, hearing is a
scent I touch. Is a sound I taste. Regular
death. With my monthly fingers. Or maybe a
new pulse. A bare foot. Tenting the skin of my
belly.

I am certain on one thing___my womb
will be allowed to tell creation stories. And
privately.

My womb has never liked the bagless
hoover. Makes her see. Dirt. She would clean
blind rather than look at what we've made
happen. Dammit, /she says.

My womb has asked. When? Will? the
birth-altar become a welcome position for all
hands?

Disappointment inks me like the
escape of apples into wet grass. It seems that
always and forever the cost of touch is
growth. But one cannot disagree;

Without human touch, there would be
no human life. When I hear this. I imagine the worm
tenting the waxy skin of the apple.
.

it is me who holds the world in me
it is me who is more than

On really bad days. Mud can be unthinkingly alarming.

I try to concentrate on the colours contained in blood. In the red. In debt. In arrears. Overdrawn. Showing a loss. I pinch myself.

Skin feels real enough in a pinch. At a push. In dire straits. Bit of a crisis. I pinch harder. My actual. Immediate. Hereness. As in not-avatar. As in not-simulacrum. As in aches.

I retreat to the garden where I'm embroidering my own shroud. My life is about all life now. My head and neck yours. My torso and arms yours. My legs and feet yours. Red thread running towards each hand-made imprint of my corpse. Like I'm a heavy dowry.

How many faulty cystic blossomings make a not-baby? That innermost burst of not-footsteps I cannot wholly abandon;

Sore prize this not-baby. Blood darkens under me with each shocking not-birth.

My life soaks the ground as I grow. Limp. Listless, doctor.

He stretches out his hand; if this growth was a baby you'd have positive feelings.

He perceives me; your feelings are negative because there is no baby, just an invasion.

He reassures me; do not worry, maintenance will powerwash the staining.

He considers also; all children are parasites, that's what I tell my own ha ha ha.

I open my mouth; my children are not parasites. I gird; that. is. simply. not. true.

He speaks directly; good god will you calm down!

There's a scalpel mind inside me that could release his clenching jaw. His remains. Would be nothing more than a dilapidated overcoat to these tar years.

All the same. The not-baby-but-
invasion has a sense of humour. Jack-in-the-
box when I want to sleep. Ride my
bike. Take a walk. Sit. In any sense, this
growth is my breviary for pain.

And if I were choosing. The colour of
wisdom would be a cellscape of joys and
sorrows. With flecks of an aftercolour
we cannot name___we do not know it yet.

in the garden
where only diabolical nature will do
all my ladders are too short

Soil may have become an enclosed
exotic. Eking out a living. In another kind of
nature. Where even children have widow weeds;

My young. Even if they. Never know
uprooted. Will never dare rest both eyes
under the bare bulb of summer;

Leaves. If there are any. Mimicking the
sound of rain. Longing. Leaves. If there are
any. Shredded by the rain that comes after
their song;

Swipe. Soil. Unmanageable soil
Difficult soil. Swipe. Wayward soil. Crooked
soil. Fractious soil. Swipe disobedient. Swipe
wilful. Perverse swipe soil. Obstinate soil.
Swipe swipe swipe. Sectioned soil.

Go to the earthworm you sluggard.
Consider her ways. And be wise;

Frost reminds me that no gardener is
understood by the ground. Frozen soil will
not give a spadeful. Even a gardener with prongs
cannot be persuasive in this situation;

Soil shall silences grow.

which earthworm if rendered vocal
would politic and preach like me?
in all vanity!

      Chasing her watery children, the worm weeps over blackbirds and ice;

      And when her motherly insight needs the sassy truth of weeds, her children's disruptions become tiny porches. For things that have no fellowship in the nosy kerfuffle of daytime.

      And I have withheld nothing. I thought we had come so far. Made a garden contented. Truth littering the lawn like leaves we could rake up. Could collect them all. Stuff bags with truths. And call ourselves prepared;

      Made us ponds with decorative solar pumps; built patios and shoffices;

      Made us great works, of earth and avocado orchards; moved water and drained valleys;

      Made us pergolas and hot-tubs; razed hillsides and planted forests of sameness;

      Meanwhile the five-faced lops and prunes and the world splits. And the worm? She still walks as a war;

  And when she parleys with him now,
they are carefully raw.

the garden is first of all native to the place

And who knows the fool from the wise? But. Maybe the five-faced have been tolerated. Not adored.

In this newshour of acceleration. The last bee. Makes vain bracelet shapes like air-glitter. The wax hate of this bee implores us to gaze___to look past our present necroscape. To imagine a future sweet in honey and care.

And still those five-faced monsters refuse with their blind, nettled language of sales.

With that, I'm so swiftly and so thickly relieved of my mind___my body sees itself slip from its exhausted root. A red flutter. No more than a whisper of pain. As all the petals fall. In unison.

Please, and with words as soft as a beard of camel's hair, tell me the calming joy of unimportant things and I will keep a crypt petalled with the stained glass and carvings of all you spill.

*as the darkest place is lit
by gentle starting light
we are born again*

Earthworms, surface little ditchers! Give me your little kisses! All the things we should have done and never did we will do. Bright as hawks.

Pray now. That in soil, there lives a spirit of forgiveness

… and there should have been wailing…

oh darling worm, let the world be right again! Let the soil turn up like it used to. To shudder its gauzy alum in basic mole brown.

Whosoever can do life anymore, will ever gasp in delight. Ever feel joy flutter in belly and hips. In places that had become so hollow.

Let earthworms give their surfacing into the beak of each day! Let furrow bees furrow furrows! Let field bees be field because;

I can't take anything with me. Into days so hot and flyless. Then flies. Sticking everywhere and on me.

*at night I might brush the backs of my fingers over
my muddy cheek
hmmmm
still here*

Brushing dirt back and forth on the path. Tidy up. At the end of a productive day in The Garden of Our Abundant Time on Earth;

We might name ourselves A Wonder That Arrived and Left.

Soil and plants have served the needs of humans. In the service of humans. And that time has come to an end:

I try to imagine the shape of maybe a small cluster. Nodding heads. A picture of generations. And I imagine that in their memory I am what? A desk? A womb? An illness? A spade?

Womb is how I can't stay within a theory of language without a *you* in it. You. Sounds like the sob I'd sob if I un-spoke that part.

I know my child. I fuss and nurse my child. Watch how they leave the house. I study their gait;

See how soil wants us to leave. Also wants us not to. A beloved silhouette she may or may not see again. In this bittersweet parting. She is fixing the shape of us in her memory.

Epilogue: the vanity of all human courses

       Beyond the garden. Sky-brought water
is a shuffle of feet. A soft-close door;

       The unoffending foot of wind presses
fenland flat. Soil lies dazed and tangled.
Gazing at the sky, as heavy as if it had bags of
flour on its little flat chest;

       And rain falls with such laziness
it's summer. And might make a downpour, or
might just mooch on

Notes & Acknowledgements

She Finds It Difficult To Pray first appeared in EcoTheo Review and *April is High Summer in 2057* in Prototype 3.

She Finds It Difficult To Pray: Etheldreda was Queen of Northumberland and founded a monastery for nuns and monks in Ely in 673 after fleeing her second husband when he reneged on their pre-nup that she could remain a virgin. In a dramatic chase, he is said to have turned back only when divine intervention whipped up a storm-surge that cut his army off. Etheldreda and her entourage of women continued to the Isle of Ely which was her dowry from her father King Anna of East Anglia. In Ely she founded the abbey that would become a cathedral. It was not uncommon for noble women to be granted chastity in marriages that were political while they pursued their religious devotion. St Etheldreda's relics are renowned for healing diseases of the throat and neck.
East Anglian dialect: wilk - to be turbulent; skeet - quick; reeve - to destroy or seize, violently

Still Moving opens with a reference to W. S. Graham, "Do not think you have to say / Anything back, But you do / Say something back which I / Hear by the way I speak to you." An early version of *Still Moving* emerged from Jos Smith's stellar Poetry Of Place module at UEA. Thank you to Anthony Anaxagorou for your line-editing, you emboldened me to find the pace *Still Moving* needed.

Womb Proverbs rejects the King James Bible as remembered and misremembered. For me, the divisive violence espoused in some verses enables unacceptable attitudes to persist, with far reaching consequences for women and minorities.

I could not have written this collection without the work of Alice Notley, Jorie Graham and Kaveh Akbar, thank you for all

I've learnt from your courageous poetry. Thank you to Clare Whistler and Kay Syrad who inspired and mentored me as kin'd & kin'd, you've shaped my work in profound ways.

Gratitude to all my poetry sisters in The 57 Collective for your love and for teaching me so much, Chaucer Cameron, Rachel Goodman, Elizabeth Lewis Williams, Jess Mookherjee, Cheryl Moskowitz, Joanna Nissel, Ilse Pedler, Elvire Roberts, Katherine Stansfield, Christina Thatcher, Hilary Watson, Clare Whistler and Jane Wilkinson. Special thanks to Rachel and Elvire for your meticulous reading (and for banishing my slapstick rakes); to Clare for encouraging me to get mucky (there will be lots more of that!); and JLM Morton for essential critiques on that first draft, thank you. Love to my family for being home, to Fen my earth-mother and to Earth, I miss you even though I barely know you yet.

Thank you to the Arts Council DYCP grant which enabled me to pay for mentoring and, crucially, time to complete my strange love poems to soil.

Praise for *Kiss My Earth*

Kiss My Earth tends to the interface of poetic language and water, human language and earthy life forms. Her sensitivity and fluent, lively intelligence interrogate what it means to be a mother during an era of complex and mounting crises. *Kiss my Earth* has a wild, womanly energy, rooted in previous generations' wisdom. The writing is accomplished and haunting, "attending fully to the business of/ being", "the rain/ that pelts my mind today", and also heart-wrenching and urgent "you cannot hear plants preach/ if you believe they do not speak". This collection resists singular interpretations, and uncorroborated, complacent hopefulness. *Kiss My Earth* is seeped in love: for the body, the community of the living, and the earth. —Jenny Pagdin

Kiss My Earth is a kind of poetic summoning: a full-throated, impassioned storm of language, with whirling eddies and moments of calm, meticulously and lovingly crafted to raise the "miracle/ we need to heal". Rooted in the earth, and the love that binds us, this is poetry of, and for, a planet in menopause. —Elizabeth Lewis Williams

Alice Willitts is a poet of extraordinary linguistic inventiveness and emotional depth. These poems are born of black fen soil but stretch to the cosmos, they are rooted in womb and mother but ask questions of society and a future where what we know has been sunk and is reimagined. *Kiss my Earth* feels both contemporary and ancient but above all a collection that is essential for our time. — Ilse Pedler

Alice Willitts is a plantswoman from The Fens; created and leads The 57 Poetry Collective; is creator and editor of the plantable poetry project DIRT; edited *Magma 78* on the theme of Collaborations; is a founding member of the biodiversity project On The Verge Cambridge. *Kiss My Earth* is her second full collection.

Poetry publications:
Something Light Written (Elephant Press, 2023), co-authored with Clare Whistler and an oak tree.
With Love, (winner of the Live Canon collection competition, 2020).
Dear, (winner of the 2018 Magma pamphlet competition).

Non-fiction:
Think Thing: an ecopoetry practice (Elephant Press, 2021).
Food Allergy and Your Child: a practical guide for parents (Class, 2007), co-authored with Deborah Carter.